D1710487

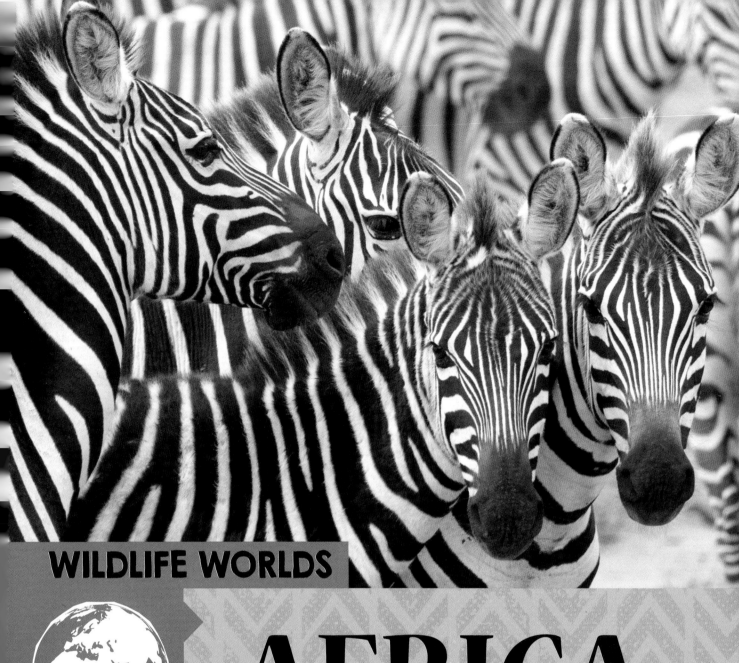

WILDLIFE WORLDS

AFRICA

TIM HARRIS

CRABTREE
PUBLISHING COMPANY
WWW.CRABTREEBOOKS.COM

CRABTREE
PUBLISHING COMPANY
WWW.CRABTREEBOOKS.COM

Published in Canada
Crabtree Publishing
616 Welland Avenue
St. Catharines, ON
L2M 5V6

Published in the United States
Crabtree Publishing
PMB 59051
350 Fifth Ave, 59th Floor
New York, NY 10118

Published in 2020 by Crabtree Publishing Company

First published in Great Britain in 2019 by The Watts Publishing Group
Copyright © The Watts Publishing Group 2019

Printed in the U.S.A./122019/CG20191101

With thanks to the Nature Picture Library

Author: Tim Harris

Editorial director: Kathy Middleton

Editors: Amy Pimperton, Robin Johnson

Series Designer: Nic Davies smartdesignstudio.co.uk

Photo researchers: Rachelle Morris (Nature Picture Library),
  Laura Sutherland (Nature Picture Library), Diana Morris

Proofreader: Wendy Scavuzzo

Production coordinator and prepress: Tammy McGarr

Print coordinator: Katherine Berti

Every attempt has been made to clear copyright.
Should there be any inadvertent omission,
please apply to the publisher for rectification.

Photo credits:
Alamy: Blickwinkel 2t, 28; Eric Nathan 6-7.
Nature PL: Eric Baccega 23bl; Jim Clare 21cr; Christophe Courteau
2b, 10-11; John Downer 12-13c; Nick Garbutt 14c, 15bl, 19tl; Edwin
Giesbers 15br; Tony Heard 10bl; Klien & Hubert 15t; Denis Huot
17l, 20, 31t; Jabruson 22t, 22bl; Roy Mangersnes 13tr, 30t; Juan
Carlos Muñoz front cover b, 9b; Inaki Relazon 29c; Anup Shah: 17br;
Enrique Lopez-Tapia 9tr; Kim Taylor 11br; Staffen Widstrand 18-19c.
Shutterstock: African Wildcat 6bl; Andrew Allport 7tr; Alslutsky
23br; AndreaAnita back cover tcl, 1t, 5br, 19tr; Selim B 27tl;
Stefano Barzellott 14bl; Radek Borovka 8c; Richard Boycott
7bl; Seyms Brugger front cover t, 3br, 19br; Volodymyr Burdiak
16;davemhuntphotography 25tl; Jon Duncan back cover tl, 3tr, 24;
Evenfh 11tl; Michael Fitzsimmons 5tr, 25tr; Peter Fodor back cover
tr; Mike Gatt back cover tcr, 21br; Homo Cosmicos 4-5bg, 26-27c;
Anton Ivanov 11bl, 32t; Andrea Izzotti 9tl; Tomas Kotouc 8bl; Serguei
Koultchitskii 21l; Andrzej Kubik 4br, 17tr; Ivan Marjanovic 3cr, 29t;
Martin Mecnarowski 27br; Anna Om 17cr, 30t; Angela N Perryman
7br; Patrick Poendl 26bl; Ondrej Prosicky 23tr; Cheryl Ramalho 4cr,
32br; Reptiles4all 27bl; Thomas Retterath 13tl; Jane Rix 25b.

Library and Archives Canada Cataloguing in Publication

Title: Africa / Tim Harris.
Names: Harris, Tim (Ornithologist), author.
Description: Series statement: Wildlife worlds |
  Previously published: London: Franklin Watts, 2019. | Includes index.
Identifiers: Canadiana (print) 2019020057X |
  Canadiana (ebook) 201902005788 |
  ISBN 9780778776772 (hardcover) |
  ISBN 9780778776833 (softcover) |
  ISBN 9781427125316 (HTML)
Subjects: LCSH: Animals—Africa—Juvenile literature. | LCSH: Habitat
  (Ecology)—Africa—Juvenile literature. | LCSH: Natural history—Africa—
  Juvenile literature. | LCSH: Africa—Juvenile literature.
Classification: LCC QL336 .H37 2020 | DDC j591.96—dc23

Library of Congress Cataloging-in-Publication Data

Names: Harris, Tim (Ornithologist), author.
Title: Africa / Tim Harris.
Description: New York : Crabtree Publishing Company, 2020. |
  Series: Wildlife worlds | Includes index.
Identifiers: LCCN 2019043968 (print) | LCCN 2019043969 (ebook) |
  ISBN 9780778776772 (hardcover) |
  ISBN 9780778776833 (paperback) |
  ISBN 9781427125316 (ebook)
Subjects: LCSH: Animals--Africa--Juvenile literature. | Plants--Africa--
  Juvenile literature.
Classification: LCC QL336 .H336 2020 (print) | LCC QL336 (ebook) |
  DDC 591.96--dc23
LC record available at https://lccn.loc.gov/2019043968
LC ebook record available at https://lccn.loc.gov/2019043969

Contents

African Continent

Africa is the second-largest continent. It is almost completely surrounded by water: the Mediterranean Sea, Atlantic Ocean, Red Sea, and Indian Ocean. A little more than half of Africa lies north of the **equator**.

Africa is a continent of rich variety. It rarely rains in the Sahara **Desert**, where daytime temperatures can rise to about 122 degrees Fahrenheit (50 °C). Not everywhere is dry and hot, however. The village of Debundscha in Cameroon is one of the wettest places on Earth, receiving more than 33 feet (10 m) of rain each year. There are even frozen glaciers on some mountains in East Africa, including Mount Kilimanjaro.

The vast Sahara Desert occupies much of the northern part of the continent.

GORILLA

GIRAFFE

Two of the world's longest rivers are found in Africa: the Nile and the Congo.

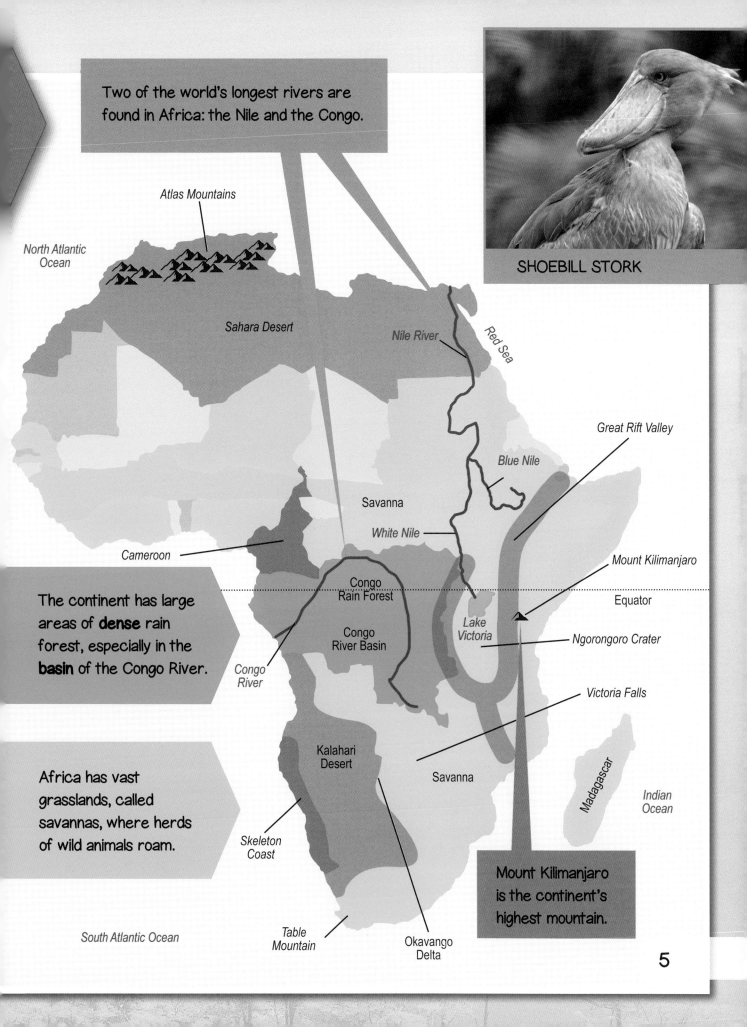

SHOEBILL STORK

North Atlantic Ocean

Atlas Mountains

Sahara Desert

Nile River

Red Sea

Great Rift Valley

Blue Nile

Savanna

White Nile

Mount Kilimanjaro

Cameroon

Equator

The continent has large areas of **dense** rain forest, especially in the **basin** of the Congo River.

Congo Rain Forest

Congo River Basin

Congo River

Lake Victoria

Ngorongoro Crater

Victoria Falls

Kalahari Desert

Madagascar

Indian Ocean

Africa has vast grasslands, called savannas, where herds of wild animals roam.

Savanna

Skeleton Coast

Mount Kilimanjaro is the continent's highest mountain.

South Atlantic Ocean

Table Mountain

Okavango Delta

Table Mountain

Looming 3,563 feet (1,086 m) above the South African city of Cape Town, Table Mountain gets its name from its flat top and very steep sides. There are amazing views over the Atlantic Ocean from the **summit** of the mountain.

Table Mountain is made of hard **sandstone** that is millions of years old. The rocks were formed in an ancient valley and then lifted high by movements of the Earth's **crust**. A "tablecloth" of clouds often rests on top of the mountain. It forms when wind carrying water from the ocean rises over the mountain and cools. The moisture allows an amazing variety of wildflowers to grow on the mountain.

Flowers bloom on Table Mountain all year, but the mix of colors changes with the seasons. There may be pink-and-white proteas (left), purple-and-yellow sorrels, and other red, orange, blue, and white flowers.

Cape sugarbirds (right), butterflies, and beetles visit flowers that grow on Table Mountain to feed on **nectar**.

TABLECLOTH

Table Mountain ghost frogs live in streams that flow down the mountain. They are found nowhere else on Earth.

Rock hyraxes travel up and down the steep slopes in search of plants, insects, lizards, and bird eggs to eat.

Skeleton Coast

The sandy coastline that runs between the cold Atlantic Ocean and the dry Namib Desert in Namibia is named the Skeleton Coast. The region got its name because people once hunted large numbers of whales and seals there, and the animal bones littered the shore. Today, the remains of shipwrecks slowly decay there.

The coast separates two very different worlds. The waters offshore are full of life, including fish, dolphins, seals, and seabirds. Inland is a vast landscape of orange and red sand **dunes**. Some can reach 980 feet (300 m) high! There are shrubs, but no trees. The only animals found there are those that can survive with very little fresh water. They include scorpions, snakes, lizards, and antelope.

Cape fur seals hunt fish in the sea. They come onto shore to rest.

The cold waters of the Benguela **Current** flow north, close to the coast. The current cools the wind passing over it, and thick fog forms in the damp air. Many ships have lost their way in the fog and run into the shore.

Great white sharks patrol the cold waters in search of **prey**.

Namib sand geckos burrow into the sand during the day and come out to hunt insects at night.

Gemsbok are powerful antelope with two long, thin horns. Females roam the sand dunes in herds.

Okavango Delta

The Okavango River flows from the highlands of Angola and into the Kalahari Desert, but it never reaches the ocean. Instead, it ends up in a flat, swampy area of Botswana called the Okavango **Delta**.

From May to September, the river fills the delta with water. The water attracts thousands of animals. Buffalo, elephants, antelope, and birds visit—along with the leopards, lions, and hyenas that hunt them. Many of the animals come to **breed** and raise their young. When the floodwaters drain away, the animals move on.

Large herds of African elephants visit the Okavango Delta for its **lush** plants.

African fish eagles swoop down from trees to grab fish from the water's surface.

Hippos (as on page 25) spend most of their time in water, only coming out at **dusk** to feed on grass.

Part of the Okavango Delta is protected in the Moremi Game Reserve. People of the BaTawana tribe live in this area of woodland, **marshes**, grassland, and lakes.

In marshy areas, dropwing dragonflies perch on tall, thin grasses called reeds.

Victoria Falls

On the border between Zimbabwe and Zambia, the waters of the mighty Zambezi River thunder over a cliff and into a deep **chasm**. This is Victoria Falls, the largest waterfall in the world. It is twice the height of Niagara Falls.

Before it reaches the waterfall, the Zambezi flows over tough, volcanic rock called basalt. Huge cracks in the basalt were once filled with soft rock called sandstone. Over thousands of years, the force of the river has worn away the sandstone, creating a **gorge** more than 5,600 feet (1,708 m) wide and 354 feet (108 m) deep.

The force of the water plunging into the chasm can be heard far away, and it throws up a cloud of mist that can be seen many miles away. That is why the local Kalolo-Lozi people called the falls Mosi-oa-Tunya, or "the smoke that thunders."

Waterbuck live along the Zambezi River. Only the males have horns.

Blood lilies grow in the damp, shady forests near Victoria Falls.

Madagascar

Located in the Indian Ocean off the east coast of Africa, Madagascar is the fourth-largest island in the world. Many of its plants and animals, including lemurs and fossas, are found nowhere else on Earth.

Madagascar's eastern side is covered by dense and lush **tropical** rain forests. For eight months of the year, the western side is bone-dry. The only plants that grow there are those that can survive the yearly **drought**. Baobab trees store water in their trunks, and acacia trees have very long **taproots** to reach water far below the surface. When the rains begin in November, the countryside becomes greener.

Tsingy de Bemaraha Strict Nature Reserve has an amazing landscape of savanna, undisturbed forest, and needle-shaped rocks called tsingy (below). Fish eagles hunt in the reddish-brown waters of the Manambolo River, while lemurs (right) live in the forest.

Giant baobab trees can grow to heights of up to 98 feet (30 m).

The Malagasy giant chameleon lives in trees, where it preys on large insects.

The fossa is a catlike **carnivore** that hunts both day and night.

Great Rift Valley

The Great **Rift** Valley runs for thousands of miles from the Red Sea in the north to the coast of Mozambique in the south. The valley has been forming for 35 million years along a line where Earth's crust is very slowly splitting apart. The first humans are believed to have lived in this valley.

There are dozens of volcanoes along the Great Rift Valley, as well as many shallow, **mineral**-rich lakes such as Nakuru and Bogoria. These lakes are called soda lakes because they are very **alkaline** like baking soda. Lake Nakuru is ideal for wading birds, such as the hundreds of thousands of long-legged pink flamingos that live there.

LESSER FLAMINGOS

Giraffes eat the high leaves and twigs on acacia trees.

Rhinos feed on grasses in the bottom of the valley by the shore. The valley's steep sides are home to vultures and birds of prey.

GREAT RIFT VALLEY

Ngorongoro Crater

In the northeastern part of Tanzania's vast savanna lies the Ngorongoro **Crater**. It is all that remains of a huge volcano that exploded and collapsed more than two million years ago.

The inside of the crater is now a wide open grassland that provides lush feeding for tens of thousands of animals. Buffalo, zebras, wildebeests, gazelles, and elephants feed there. In May, early in the dry season, huge herds of wildebeests leave the crater in search of fresh grasses and water. They are often accompanied by zebras and gazelles. The animals return at the start of the rainy season in November.

The rim of the gigantic Ngorongoro Crater rises 2,000 feet (610 m) above the crater floor. Rivers flow into a shallow lake in the lowest part of the crater, and animals that stay during the dry season gather there.

These wildebeests and zebras are starting their yearly **migration** north.

The Ngorongoro Crater has one of the highest **concentrations** of lions in East Africa.

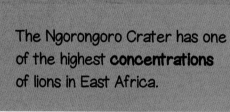

Mount Kilimanjaro

Kilimanjaro is a **dormant** volcano that towers high over the plains of Tanzania. At 19,341 feet (5,895 m) above sea level, it is Africa's highest mountain. Despite being close to the equator, its summit is bitterly cold, especially at night. It snows frequently on Kilimanjaro, and there is always ice near the summit.

Few large animals live on the higher parts of Mount Kilimanjaro. Below the icy summit and above the **tree line**, there is **moorland** and cold desert. Forests grow lower on the mountain and provide homes for birds, colobus monkeys, and African elephants. In recent years, thousands of trees have been planted on the lower slopes to reduce soil **erosion**.

Mount Kilimanjaro is made up of three **volcanic cones**. One of the volcanic cones is named Kibo. It has openings, called fumaroles, which release hot gases from deep underground. Kibo has not erupted for thousands of years, but it could again someday.

Black-and-white colobus monkeys have extremely long tails.

While feeding on nectar, sunbirds **pollinate** flowers that grow on the mountain.

Giant lobelias are slow-growing plants found on Kilimanjaro's upper slopes.

Congo Rain Forest

The Congo is the second-largest rain forest on Earth. Located in the basin of the Congo River in Central Africa, this massive rain forest stretches across six countries and is 772,200 square miles (2 million square km) in size. Only the Amazon rain forest in South America is larger.

The Congo rain forest is home to more than 11,000 different kinds of plants. Some of the forest is so dense that it has probably never been explored by people. Scientists think that many thousands of beetles and bugs that no one has ever seen live there. The rain forest is drained by massive rivers, including the Congo, Lomami, and Ubangi. People have cut down parts of the forest for its wood, or to make space for farms and towns.

OKAPI

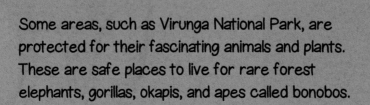

Some areas, such as Virunga National Park, are protected for their fascinating animals and plants. These are safe places to live for rare forest elephants, gorillas, okapis, and apes called bonobos.

Despite their fearsome appearance, mountain gorillas eat mostly fruit and leaves, as well as a few insects.

White-crested hornbills are large birds that live in the Congo rain forest.

African giant swallowtails are some of the largest butterflies in the world. Their wings measure 9 inches (23 cm) from tip to tip.

Nile River

The Nile is the world's longest river. It flows 4,132 miles (6,650 km) through mountains, deserts, lush **oases**, and marshes. It begins at Lake Victoria in Uganda and flows north all the way to the coast of Egypt, where its waters enter the Mediterranean Sea.

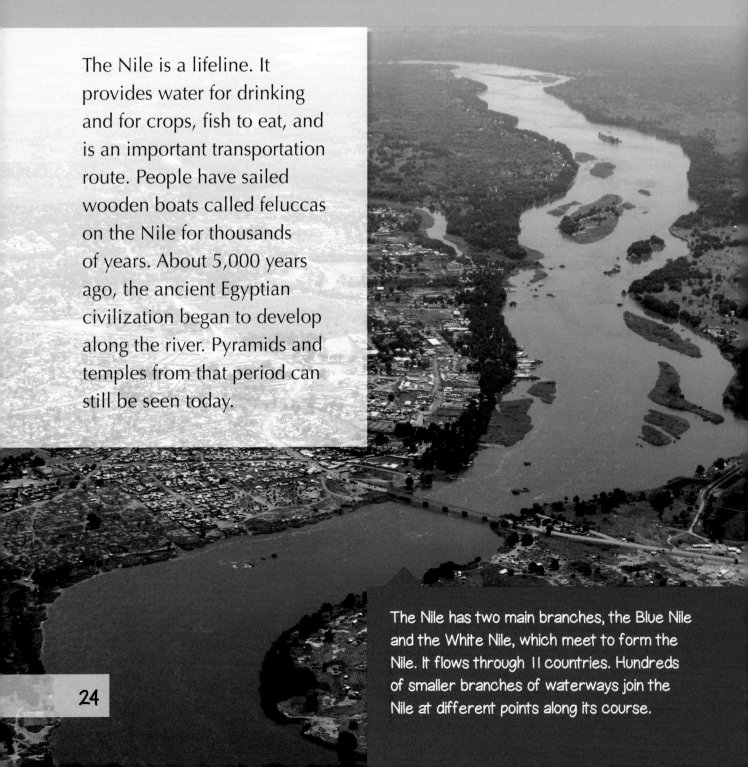

The Nile is a lifeline. It provides water for drinking and for crops, fish to eat, and is an important transportation route. People have sailed wooden boats called feluccas on the Nile for thousands of years. About 5,000 years ago, the ancient Egyptian civilization began to develop along the river. Pyramids and temples from that period can still be seen today.

The Nile has two main branches, the Blue Nile and the White Nile, which meet to form the Nile. It flows through 11 countries. Hundreds of smaller branches of waterways join the Nile at different points along its course.

Nile crocodiles are fierce **predators** that can grow up to 20 feet (6 m) in length.

The shoebill stork uses its large beak to catch fish, frogs, small snakes, and even baby crocodiles.

Hippos often fight to defend their **territories**. Their huge size makes them very dangerous.

Sahara Desert

Stretching from the Red Sea in the east to the Atlantic Ocean in the west, the vast Sahara is the world's largest desert. It is bigger than the United States. Some areas are covered by fields of sand dunes that are constantly being moved by the wind. Other regions are stony or rocky.

The Sahara is a difficult place for animals to survive. It is baking hot during the day, and sometimes freezing cold at night. There is little water and often no plant life. Despite these harsh conditions, many animals live there. Most avoid the burning sunlight during the day by hiding in cracks between rocks or burying themselves in the sand. At night when it is cooler, they come out to feed and hunt.

For thousands of years, desert people have used dromedary camels to carry heavy loads.

The Sahara sand viper is a **venomous** snake that buries itself in the sand so it can **ambush** prey and stay cool!

In the mountains of Tassili du Hoggar, in the central Sahara, there are sandstone peaks that have been shaped by the wind. The Tuareg people have lived in this area for thousands of years. It has green oases and ancient rock paintings.

The Western Sand Sea, or erg, in northern Algeria is one of the most **barren** places on Earth. There are no permanent villages, no roads, and no plants there. Everything is covered with enormous sand dunes.

The fennec fox keeps cool by losing heat through its very large ears. It usually hunts at night.

27

Atlas Mountains

The Atlas Mountains lie in the far north of Africa between the Mediterranean Sea and the Sahara Desert. The mountain range is rich in natural resources. Trees are grown for timber on the forested lower slopes, and copper, salt, and even silver are found deep underground.

There are many **ridges** covered with forests of oak, cedar, and fir trees in the Atlas Mountains. The ridges are separated by valleys and steep-sided gorges that rivers tumble through. Higher up in the mountains, the forests thin out and are replaced with meadows, which are warm in summer but very cold in winter. In spring and summer, the meadows come alive with wildflowers and butterflies.

Mount Toubkal is the highest peak in the Atlas Mountains, rising more than 13,670 feet (4,167 m) above sea level. Many hikers make the long climb to its rocky summit in spring and summer. In winter, the higher slopes are covered with snow.

A great variety of butterflies are found there, including the Spanish festoon (left), Moroccan marbled white, and common tiger blue.

Barbary macaques are monkeys that live in groups called troops in forested parts of the Atlas Mountains.

Glossary

alkaline Containing salts that neutralize acids

ambush Attack by surprise

barren Having few or no plants

basin Land from which water flows into a river

breed Produce babies

carnivore An animal that eats other animals

chasm A deep, steep-sided hole or opening in the ground

concentrations Large numbers of something in one place

crater A bowl-shaped hole around a volcano, or where a volcano once was

crust Earth's outer layer

current Water that is moving in one direction

delta Where a river drops mud and sand as it enters a lake or ocean

dense Growing close together

desert A place that receives little or no rainfall and has few or no plants

dormant Not active for now

drought A long period without rain

dunes Hills of sand piled up by the wind

dusk Sunset

equator An imaginary line around Earth that is an equal distance from the North and South poles

erosion The process by which rocks or soil are worn away

gorge A narrow valley with steep-sided walls and usually a stream

lush Growing thick and healthy

marshes Areas of soft, wet land with many grasses and other plants

migration The act of moving from one region to another with the seasons

mineral A substance such as salt that is formed naturally under the ground

moorland An open, hilly area with low-lying plants

nectar A sugary liquid found in flowers

oases Fertile areas with water in a desert

pollinate To carry pollen from one flower to another, allowing seeds to be made

predators Animals that hunt and eat other animals

prey Animals that are eaten by other animals

ridges Long areas of land at the top of a mountain

rift A crack or split

sandstone Rock made of grains of sand or quartz that have been pressed together over time

summit The very top

taproots Roots that grow straight down

territories Areas that some animals defend during the breeding season

tree line An imaginary line on a mountain that no trees can grow above

tropical Relating to the tropics, the areas above and below the equator

venomous Producing chemicals that can injure or kill prey

volcanic cone A triangle-shaped hill that forms around the opening of a volcano

Further Information

Books

Hudak, Heather C. *Pathways Through Africa*. Crabtree Publishing, 2019.

Koontz, Robin. *Learning About Africa*. LernerClassroom, 2015.

Rockett, Paul. *Mapping Africa*. Crabtree Publishing, 2017.

Wanner, Zukiswa. *Africa*. Children's Press, 2019.

Websites

www.dkfindout.com/us/earth/continents/africa/
This website has lots of interesting and fun facts about Africa.

www.ducksters.com/geography/africa.php
Discover profiles of every country in Africa.

http://gowild.wwf.org.uk/regions/africa-fact-files
Learn more about your favorite animals in these WWF fact files.

www.nationalgeographic.com/animals/index/
Type in the names of animals and get lots of fascinating facts about mammals, reptiles, amphibians, fish, and birds.

Index